Digital Marketing

For Business Growth

The Essential Guide To Digital Marketing For Businesses

Scott Jones

About The Author

Scott Jones is the founder and CEO of a successful and growing digital marketing agency – 123 Internet Group. For over 15 years he has built a team of digital marketing champions who support the growing demand in this space.

The services of this leading full service digital marketing agency include design, web development, search engine marketing, social media management and digital strategy.

During COVID-19, Scott navigated the global pandemic providing continued support to local, national and international clients - without the need to furlough any staff or receive grants for support. 123 Internet Group continued to thrive and expanded, employing new team members from within the industry. The global landscape changed, but the requirement for digital services continued to boom.

In this book, Scott shares some of the fundamentals surrounding the digital marketing topic and explains how each of the core components connect to create a 360 degree approach to success.

CONTENTS

INTRODUCTION

This book will enable you to understand and harness the power of Digital Marketing as a core driver in the marketing strategy for your organisation. You will understand the foundation principles of Digital Marketing, and be able to distinguish how it differs from traditional marketing.

Internet, in today's world has opened the gateway of tremendous digital marketing opportunities for any size of organisation. By utilising different channels of digital marketing, organisations cannot just share their product and services online; additionally, they can gain clients, entice them and can convert them to boost their ROI. The speed and straightforwardness with which the digital media transmits data and supports anorganisation is astonishing. In this book, every single aspect of Digital Marketing will be discussed to help you understand what Digital Marketing is, how it functions, and how it can help optimise your next marketing campaigns.

According to Internet World Stats (www.internetworld-stats.com) there are now 3,885,567,619 internet users across the globe. The world is super-connected nowadays and all things considered, marketing and advertising have changed dramatically. This is particularly valid because of the ascent of social media networks, which has changed how organisations speak with potential and existing customers.

So, before we find out about all the various aspects of Digital Marketing, let's find out precisely what Digital Marketing is and what does it incorporate? Essentially, it is an aggregate term, which is utilised where advertising and marketing meet web innovation and different types of online media platforms. Let's firstly throw some light on the basics of Digital Marketing via the definition given below; this is the first step in our journey to uncover Digital Marketing and what it means right now.

CHAPTER 1

INTRODUCTION TO DIGITAL MARKETING

Digital Marketing Definition

Wikipedi's definition of Digital Marketing states: "Digital marketing is the marketing of products or services using digital technologies, mainly on the Internet, but also including mobile phones, display advertising, and any other digital medium."

When we look at this in more detail, Digital Marketing should be understood as a well-targeted, conversion-oriented, quantifiable, and interactive marketing of products or services by utilising digital innovation to achieve customers, and transform them into clients in a sustainable fashion.

The whole concept and functionalities of Digital Marketing are more competent, effective, result-oriented and measurable, which make it very different from traditional marketing.

The traditional way of marketing lets organisations market their products or services on printed media, radio and TV commercials, billboards, business cards, and in numerous other comparable ways where Internet or web-based social networking sites were not utilised for promoting.

However, traditional promoting approaches had constrained client reachability and lacked the ability of driving clients' purchasing conduct. In addition, traditional marketing methods were not quantifiable too. Let us understand noticeable difference between Traditional Marketing & Digital Marketing.

Difference Between Traditional Marketing & Digital Marketing

Traditional Marketing

1. Communication is unidirectional in traditional marketing, which means, an organisation communicates its services to its audiences.

2. The medium of communication in traditional marketing is generally printed, phone calls, emails, and letters.

3. The campaign in Traditional marketing takes more time as designing, preparing, and launching is involved.

4. It is best for reaching a local audience.

5. It is almost impossible to measure the effectiveness of a traditional marketing campaign.

Digital Marketing

1. Communication is bidirectional in Digital Marketing as organisations can communicate with customers and customers can ask queries or make suggestions to businesses as well.

2. The medium of communication is more powerful and involves social media, websites, chats, apps and email.

3. Digital marketing campaigns can be developed quite rapidly and with digital tools, channelising Digital Marketing campaigns is easier.

4. It is very effective for reaching global audiences.

5. Digital Marketing lets you measure the effectiveness of a digital marketing campaign through analytics.

Digital Marketing accomplishes targets of marketing of a business through various Digital Marketing Channels.

5 Common Misconceptions About Digital Marketing

It is no doubt that in this technology-driven world, digital media based marketing has given the business development a new boosting towards faster growth. But the following are some common mistakes that a newbie should avoid:

1. Higher time consumption versus fewer results

The first thing that disappoints a beginner is time against results. It is a fact that there is hardly any shortcut to success (except pay-per-click advertisement) in the digital or the online marketing sphere! When you begin to start marketing your business online, you have to wait and watch for results for some time. After a few outcomes, refining your strategy can lead to expected results. But this does not mean that you should stop working on digital media based marketing ploys, competitors and the digital landscape changes quickly. One thing you must remember or convey to your superiors that results of digital marketing stay for a long time.

Once the flow of business beings, it does far better in revenue collection than off-line marketing processes.

2. It is too technical and hard to track or measure

We can personally tell you that we have come across people who simply try to negate digital or online marketing as it is a bit technical. Some people are even known to say things like, "You people better understand things as you have the technical know-how". But understand this now, with the introduction of Content Management Systems and east to use tools you don't need to hold some sort of technical degree. Googling around and with the support of external agencies, you can easily handle your website updates and monitor your online marketing efforts. And talking about the tracking process, there are so many tools to analyse and trace the output of your digital marketing efforts. For example, there are many keyword analysis tools that can help you know the best keywords or phrases that would help you move forward and outperform your competitors on Google search results.

3. You need to invest a lump sum of money for success

Another setback that can really affect a beginner to take the first firm step in the domain of digital or online marketing is the money issue. Some people have a big misconception that digital or online marketing means an investment of a considerable part of your total marketing budget. But this is not at all true. Whether you employ a digital marketing agency or try to do things yourself, very small nominal investment can start showing you greater results. You can expect better results from other conventional marketing ploys even. There are so many free techniques that can be implemented to get firsthand results.

4. SEO is dead so stop this nonsense

There are so many self-appointed experts who have grown some deep knowledge in themselves about Google and SEO and wil provide the misconception that Google now does not allow or adhere to conventional practices of optimisation of web pages (Meta tags, content etc.) These types of conceptions are nothing but misconceptions about digital marketing! The on-page SEO (working on Meta and content) still has importance to Google and other search engines. Those ploys guide search crawlers to index and show the best results against the user queries. Yes, SEO techniques are becoming advanced to bring the best results to the customers and it is not going to die whilst the search engines are in the market.

5. Social networking is all digital or online marketing

In this era of 'Facebook', 'Twitter', 'WhatsApp' people are growing a deep misconception in themselves. They have started to think that social media marketing is all in all in digital marketing. If you can market your business in social channels, you then do not need to do anything else. But for the beginners, stop thinking likewise! If you search, you would find there are so many other techniques that help in bringing results. Do not indulge your time entirely on social media marketing. For example, you have to know and work on making your online presence mobile friendly to reach the highest number of people who may visit your website from these platforms. And to do that, you have to know some fundamental techniques that stand as a part of digital media based marketing.

Well, there are so many other misconceptions about digital marketing processes. But we have tried to put forward only 5 mistakes that can lead a beginner to defeat! Everyone should research thoroughly and find out the truth. There are so many blogs of experts that can guide a beginner to success in digital and online marketing. For example, Google's Spokesperson Mr. Matt Cutts has a blog where he shares his good thoughts on digital and online marketing good practices. Such blogs and helps are innumerable, and following those, success is bound to come for a beginner.

6 Trends And Opportunities In Digital Marketing

2017 was a marvelous year for digital marketing. After gaining a lot of popularity with companies creating an online presence and promoting the products and services via several social media channels, it is believed that the online world is going to expand further. There are more media options than ever, new channels and formats playing a substantial role in giving your digital marketing strategy a rise in the coming year. It's time for all the marketers to review the lessons from the last year and look for new skills required for your organisation to succeed this year and beyond. Let's drill down into the key trends that should be your focus to formulate effective digital marketing.

1. Content Marketing Will Evolve

It's all about blogging, eBooks, and other content types – content marketing will continue to succeed and become more creative with visual content to break through the noise.

"In 2021, post COVID-19 content will be more unique, challenging, and thriving."

A great promotional tool for businesses, it is the perfect opportunity for the marketers to make it even bigger. In this year, we will likely to see interactive content – one of the biggest goals that help you stand out from the crowd and drives as much as engagement as possible. Also, try to focus on the practical as well. Evergreen content offers value to the audience, generating longer lasting results. So, shift your focus to driving growth in existing audiences to make specific, consistent management until conversion.

21

2. Use Of Plenty Of Big Data

Of course, everybody does, but you can use different types of data to get more attention of your target audience. Make this year a success by analysing your data productivity and Return on Investment (ROI). As customers play an enormous role in the success of a brand, Big Data makes it possible for the companies to advance customer experience. Your customers expect attention; if you are listening to their queries, then you are providing them with an enriched shopping experience. It also offers excellent opportunities to learn more about the consumers, allowing them to personalise their products and services to gain their confidence.

3. Digital Workforces To Scale Business Processes

Latest digital technologies are all around us and are growing faster than ever. If organisations use them effectively, it will generate a significant competitive advantage. This will give the employees new digital skills to adapt and render them with the most relevant platforms, tools, and motivations. Some of the technologies driving the digital workplace are production studio technology, immersive technologies, personal clouds, process hacking, and microlearning.

4. Artificial Intelligence Making Amazing Strides

One area that will continue to offer opportunities for transforming customer service is Artificial Intelligence (AI); and it is deemed to bring huge shifts in how individuals notice and interact with technology. AI is creating a smarter experience every day, from messaging platforms to imagining insights and machine learning. With the help of Artificial Intelligence, marketers are capable of understanding the human knowledge and experience. They can complete the most consuming human-actions in a fraction of a second. Moreover, this technology will make it easier to extract all the information required for marketing the brand to the targeted viewers.

5. Social Media Grow Exponentially

Customer preferences, features, and brand opportunities will continue to surprise us. There will be changes this year and beyond. As social becomes more associated, it is time for the marketers to keep their eyes on the strategies to remain ahead of the competitors. Snapchat is one of the most efficient channels for brands to connect with customers in unique ways. It offers a chance to use Geofilters efficiently to reap the benefits of a network. Create something that entices individuals, target the right audience, and then sustain the momentum with a marketing campaign to come within reach of more people. Try live video-streaming to build a strong digital marketing foundation.

6. People-Based Marketing Is In Demand

Organisations are turning to people-based marketing where ads are based on data that generates relevancy to potential customers. The performance is real: Advertisers and marketers are holding addressable media for a superb reason. 2 in 3 advertisers said that the capability to onboard customer data is vital. The main technique of implementing a people-based marketing strategy is to get a more comprehensive view of your potential consumers by amalgamating online and offline data. Doing this can genuinely reap the advantages of people based marketing campaign.

CHAPTER 2

MARKETING FUNDAMENTALS

What is marketing? Marketing is the process of interesting potential customers and clients in your products and services.

The key word in this marketing definition is "process"; marketing involves researching, promoting, selling, and distributing your products or services.

It's a vast topic, which is why there are tonnes written on marketing, and why you can take a four-year marketing degree. But essentially marketing involves everything you do to get your potential customers and your product or service together.

When you're putting together a marketing program for your business, concentrate on the basics, the four key components of any marketing plan:

• Products and services

• Promotion

• Distribution

• Pricing

The name of the game in marketing is attracting and retaining a growing base of satisfied customers. Creating and implementing a marketing plan will keep your marketing efforts focused and increase your sales.

Good marketing helps you to examine all aspects of your business, no matter how small, and think about how they affect the perception your customers' have of your business. Although, marketing takes time, research and analysis, successful marketing can help you increase your bottom line.

Here are some examples of where marketing is already evident in your business model:

• How you are positioned in the market

• Who your target audience is

• How you price your products and services

• The quality of your products.

Writing a marketing plan can help you define some aspects of your business and help you focus on your priorities.

Marketing plan

A marketing plan outlines the specific actions you intend to carry out to interest potential customers and clients in your product and service and persuade them to buy the product and services you offer.

The marketing plan implements your marketing strategy. It tells you where you want to go from here. The plan is the specific roadmap that's going to get you there. A marketing plan may be developed as a standalone document or as part of a business plan. Either way, it is a blueprint for communicating the value of your products and services to your customers.

Prior to Developing a Marketing Plan

You can't develop a marketing plan without market research. Market research guides the direction of your marketing plan, giving you vital information on your potential customers (your target market) and the feasibility of your products and services.

Market research should include monitoring industry and economic trends, scouting the competition to determine how you can gain a competitive advantage in pricing and customer service, and identifying the best ways to reach your target market via advertising and social media, etc.

What Goes Into a Marketing Plan

A typical marketing plan consists of the following sections:

Executive Summary

The executive summary is a high-level overview of the marketing plan. This section should provide a brief summary of the plan for those who may not read the entire document.

Business Description

This section describes what the business is all about, including the location, names of the business owners, the current business situation (position in the marketplace), the company mission statement and core values, and external factors that are currently affecting the business now or may do so in future.

Target Market

The section profiles the customers the business intends to target. This includes:

• The size of the market and future trends.

• Demographic information such as age, gender, religion, marital status, education level, family size, ethnic and cultural background, income levels, etc.

• Customer interests, habits, wants, and needs, and how these factors relate to a demand for the company's product(s) or service(s).

Unique Selling Proposition

The unique selling proposition describes how the company will gain a competitive advantage in the marketplace by supplying one or more of the following benefits to customers:

• Providing a unique or superior product.

- Delivering lower prices.

- Providing better customer service.

SWOT Analysis and the Competition

This section compares the company strengths, weaknesses, opportunities, and threats (known as SWOT analysis) with those of the competition, so the company can explain to customers why they should choose its products or services over those of its competitors. It also highlights areas where the business will need to improve to compete more effectively.

Distribution/Delivery Plan

Distribution and delivery outlines how the company will sell/deliver your products to customers.

Methods of sales and delivery include retail, wholesale, direct to homes or businesses, or online.

Marketing Objectives

This section describes the company marketing objectives for the near future (typically one year in advance).

Perhaps the goal is to increase sales by 25 percent by the end of the next fiscal year or achieve 40% of the market share in the local area for a specific product or service.

Marketing Action Plan

The action plan includes detailed information about the products/services to be sold, including product descriptions, benefits of the product/service versus the competition, pricing strategies, and plans for how the product/service will be promoted, whether using traditional methods of advertising or online using social media.

Budget

Lastly, the marketing budget section includes a break-down of the cost of proceeding with the marketing plan. The cost/benefit analysis demonstrates how implementing the marketing plan should result in increased sales and revenue.

8 Ways to Improve Your Small Business Marketing Process

Every small business needs a marketing plan to effectively reach and engage customers. But it doesn't end there. Once you are armed with your marketing plan, it's time to create an execution plan that will guide your entire marketing process. The tips below will help improve your marketing process, whether you're just getting started or if your current campaign has started to fizzle out.

Invest In Your Team

Don't be afraid to spend a little money on the things that really matter. Marketing should never be seen as a 'cost' to the organisation. The money you spend on marketing is an investment in the future of your business.

1. **Train Staff** - Invest in training your employees in all of the aspects of your business that are relevant to their jobs. It's also a good idea to make sure every employee has an understanding of the business and marketing goals, working together to achieve the mutual goals.

2. **Go Pro Whenever Possible** - Resist the urge to design your logo or host your website 'on the cheap' just because you think it will help you save a few pounds. Marketing shouldn't save you money; it should make you money.

3. **Hire the Right Contractors** - If you get bogged down in too many of the details, you may face burnout (and possibly waste a lot of money). Vet your contractors well, and you won't have to micromanage the entire project and processes.

Automate (When It Makes Sense)

Automation is a double-edged sword, and there is such a thing as too much automation. So, this tip comes with a caveat: use your common sense to determine which tasks should be completed by a living, breathing human being.

4. **Automate Social Content** - There are several tools out there to help you automatically publish blog links to your social media accounts. Using them will save you the hassle of manually composing and posting an update when your new content goes live.

On such tool we offer as an agency to our smaller clients can be found here: https://www.123internet.agency/social/

5. **Create Email Autoresponders** - There's no reason to write and send individual emails for repeat events.

Create autoresponders that give next steps and important information any time someone makes an online purchase, signs up for your newsletter, creates an account, or contacts you for customer service.

Keep Learning and Developing New Ideas

The fastest way to get your campaign off the ground is to study the latest trends. As you learn from others, you should be able to prioritise tasks. The more you know, the easier it will be to the choose tactics that will have the biggest, most positive impact on your success.

6. **Network** - Sit down for a coffee one-on-one, form a meet-up, or join an online group with other small business owners to discuss what works and what doesn't. You might discover some simple strategies you hadn't thought of before, and learn what tactics have been a

waste of time for others. There are many local networking groups, one of the biggest and most well known international ones is BNI – there are others if their format doesn't suit your taste.

7. **Enroll in a Webinar** - There are online classes out there for just about everything, and marketing is no exception. In many cases, enrollment is either completely free or simply requires you to create a profile.

8. **Use Available Tools** - Don't forget to scour the Internet for public resources. Check out everything you can find from YouTube videos and local government resources to marketing blogs and social media chats.

Successful small business marketing relies on having a solid marketing plan and a system for executing that plan. If you don't have a functional marketing plan yet, start here. Answering a set of key questions will give you the framework you need to create an effective marketing plan.

Finding Your Target Audience

Whether you sell washing lines or wiper blades, you need to understand your customer if you want to maximise your sales. Who are you selling to? Why should they buy your product? What do they stand to gain?

1. Understand the problems that you solve

The starting point in defining the target market for your proposition is to understand the problems that you solve. Once you have a good idea what these are, you can start to work out who is most likely to suffer from these problems.

2. Paint a picture of the customer

Start to list all the different types of customers that suffer from the problems you solve. Once done, you can start to build up a picture of these customers. Group them by location - for example, high net worth individuals tend to live in certain postcodes. Group them by market sector - are they manufacturers, recruitment agents, and so on.

Ask yourself other types of relevant questions about these people. Are they married? Are they male or female? Do they play golf? Define them in as many relevant ways as possible.

3. Who will gain from the value in your offer?

Ask yourself:

To whom will these problems be most troublesome?

Who will have the most to lose by not dealing with these issues?

If you can demonstrate that the cost of NOT sorting out the problems is GREATER than the cost of dealing with them, then your case becomes compelling.

Remember to take into account aspects like emotional upheaval, stress and the risk to reputation when implementing your solution, as well as a bottom line cost. It is all these factors that make up the value in your offering.

4. Think about your market

Today we live in the world of niche. For example, we are no longer prisoners of television schedules. We can watch what we want at our convenience from almost anywhere in the world; meaning every person can enjoy a unique viewing experience.

The web is fantastic at delivering personalised products and services, cutting out many of the distribution challenges that previously existed.

It is these factors that mean it is a more effective strategy to be a big fish in a small pond rather than the other way round. It will be easier to build your reputation and gain referrals. You will also find you get more from your marketing endeavours.

Therefore, with the previous knowledge gained, start to segment your market. Do you want to work:

With particular types of people - high net worth individuals, men, women, golfers, and so on?

In certain geographical locations – Milton Keynes, London, and so on?

Around tight market sectors - manufacturers or accountants, and so on?

5. Look internally at your company

One way of deciding on the right markets to pursue is to think about your company and your business.

Do you have particular areas of expertise? For example, do you have a lot of experience in particular markets, such as working with lawyers?

Do you have unique knowledge of a specific geographical area?

Are you better at getting on with certain types of people?

All these factors could help you establish a particularly attractive offering.

Take an accountant working alone in Northampton, for example. For a start, working all over the country is probably not practical. They may therefore decide to only work with clients within 50 miles.

It may be that before going it alone they worked in-house for a couple of different entrepreneurial businesses. Therefore, the accountant may decide to make their marketplace 'Entrepreneurs in the Midlands'.

Suddenly, if you are an entrepreneur in this catchment area, this is an accountant probably worth knowing. By solely working in this area they are more likely to introduce you to the right people and have more market knowledge of schemes and funding available to entrepreneurs.

Meanwhile, by concentrating in this marketplace, the accountant knows which websites to look at and belong to, which publications to read and possibly write for, and which networks to attend. Within this market it will be quite easy for the accountant to become known. Without limiting their market it would almost be impossible to know where to start.

6. What else is available?

Once you have decided the answers to some of these questions you must look at the market to see what else is available. The question you must have an answer to is:

Why am I uniquely placed to solve the problem?

It may be that for some marketplaces there is no answer. However, in certain sectors or geographical locations there may be a compelling response to that question.

If you are unable to answer the question, you either have the wrong target market or the wrong offering. In this case, more work will need to be done before you start targeting your potential

Identify Your Unique Selling Proposition

The Unique Selling Proposition (USP) is what sets your organisation, products and services apart from your competitors. Expressed as a single sentence that summarises the essence of your business, the Unique Selling Proposition serves as the theme of your marketing.

The question the USP answers for your customers is, "Why buy yours instead of the others?"

The catch is that the answer the Unique Selling Proposition provides must offer your potential customers a specific benefit that they see as attractive.

It's not enough to say (however many times you say it) that your product or service is "better" or has "more value". Vague-speak doesn't cut it with customers, who will want to know how and why that particular benefit will apply to them.

That's why developing a USP before you bring a product or service to market is an excellent way to determine in advance if it will sell. If there's nothing that sets your product or service apart from the competition, why will anyone want to buy it? And even if there is something that makes your product or service stand out, is it something that consumers will see as valuable? If both of these conditions are not met, why spend time or money on developing a product offering that's not viable in the marketplace?

A Unique Selling Proposition is an especially critical marketing tool for small businesses who are forced to compete with other small businesses and larger players in ther market space.

Your business may have superior service or product offerings, but unless you can get the message out to potential customers, they will have no reason to choose your business over a competitor.

History of the USP

The Unique Selling Proposition concept was created by American advertising executive Rosser Reeves (1910 to 1984).

He believed that the only purpose of advertising was to communicate a particular company's slogan for their product or service and that this slogan should remain unchanged.

How Do You Create a Unique Selling Proposition?

1) Start by reviewing your business offerings from the perspective of the target market, which may be segmented by factors such as gender, age, income level, race, religion, education, etc. In basic terms, put yourself in your potential customer's shoes!

What does your typical customer really want? Is it lower price, better customer service, location (convenience), home delivery, etc.?

2) Ask yourself, "What is it that my product or service offers that my competitors' products or services don't offer?" Then ask yourself what specific benefit this provides your customers. If you can't give exact answers to these questions in a few sentences you are probably not doing enough to differentiate your business offerings from your competitors in the marketplace.

3) Now put it all together in one sentence memorable enough to use as an advertising slogan. For example, "We serve the best gluten-free pizza in the city", or "Complete car services that you can trust", or "Top quality furniture at an affordable price".

4) Then use it - in your advertising, in your emails to customers, on your website, in social media postings on Facebook, LinkedIn, Twitter, and Pinterest, and on all other marketing and promotional materials - wherever it might get the attention of potential customers.

Speak to your existing customers regularly and get feedback on how you can improve your product or service offerings to give them more reason to choose your business rather than the competition.

Some Famous Unique Selling Proposition Examples:

Hallmark: When you care enough to send the very best.

Subway: Subs with under 6 grams of fat.

The Men's Wearhouse (George Zimmer): You're going to like the way you look - I guarantee it.

FedEx Corporation: When it absolutely, positively has to get there overnight.

One of the most famous Unique Selling Propositions that Rosser Reeves created was for M&Ms; "The milk chocolate melts in your mouth, not in your hand."

CHAPTER 3

MARKET RESEARCH

Know Your Customers

Knowing your customers and their preferences is the easiest way to customer retention.

Why know your customers? Initially, the seller-purchaser relationship was tilted in favor of the seller. This was because the competition was less and purchasers had fewer choices. However, the last two decades have seen a consistent power shift. With technological advancement and easy availability of information, the buyer now has the upper hand. If your business doesn't provide what's required, a competitor is just around the corner to grab the opportunity.

Customers today have become more demanding and expect innovative solutions. Merely meeting customer needs is not enough. The goal is to exceed their expectations so that they return to do more business with you. Studies have shown that about 80% of a company's business comes from its existing customers. In such scenario, customer retention assumes increased importance. To retain customers and ensure that they do not move on to your competitors, it is essential to understand the customer and customise your product/ service offering to suit their interests and needs.

How to get to know your customers better? Businesses today don't function like the corner shops anymore where there's face-to-face interaction with the customer everyday. Today, customers may be interacting with the business without the business even knowing about it. A visit by the customer to the business's website is an example of one such interaction. The key is to capture such interactions, understand the customers and predict their future behavior based on these interactions and use that to anticipate customer needs before they arise. This way the business will be adopting a customer-centric approach to its offering. Knowing the customers will also help your business to make smart decisions that enhance customer experience. Every decision being made can be looked at from the customer's point of view. However, for this ideal customer-centric approach to become a reality, it is also essential that the commitment towards customer focus is top-down. Only when the CEO and the Board are committed to customer relations will the other employees believe in the concept. Until your business adopts a proactive approach to customer satisfaction, this would not be easy.

What are the benefits of knowing your customers? Knowing your customers better can help you boost sales. This is because once you know what could be of potential interest to the customers, you can cross-sell or up-sell relevant product/service offerings. Also, you can save considerably on costs incurred in acquiring/ retaining a customer, since your marketing efforts would now be more focused and yield better results. Improved customer satisfaction and loyalty are some other benefits that will arise.

What are the core requirements in this process? To know your customers and be able to understand them, your business needs to adopt an integrated approach to the whole process. All the functions should be well coordinated, especially, marketing and sales. Your marketing strategies should be highly customised, running primarily on customer activities that arise as a part of client interaction. The information gathered from the customers should be stored in such a manner that it can be retrieved in a timely fashion and makes sense to all who would be using it. A good Customer Relationship Management (CRM) software package which has analytical functionality can help you with this. Without proper coordination between marketing and sales, the efforts put in by the business to know your customers can fail.

Online Surveys & Feedback

The importance of online surveys as modern marketing tools is great, as people search for almost everything they need in the online space. That is why, to thrive in business, companies rely on online surveys to learn the opinion of customers on products and services. Surveys are a tool which helps companies to obtain feedback - and feedback is essential to help to learn what should be improved, what should be altered to meet customers' expectations and needs, etc. The opinions and advice that customers give are often the basis for improvements which help to enhance products and services and match the demands of the vast public.

Another benefit of online surveys is that by offering them to customers and visitors to websites, companies can learn what new products and services are expected to meet the changing or new needs of groups of customers.

But online surveys are not beneficial for companies only. Respondents to surveys are also benefited by their participation in surveys. Often, survey filling is a paid activity, a manner of earning money for people who do that in their spare time to supplement their income. Of course, the amount of money earned depends on the frequency of participation in survey filling. People who have more spare time and willingness can join several websites where surveys are offered, or participate in surveys launched by several companies, to augment their earnings. To participate in online surveys, people need to have computers, Internet connection, email accounts, and PayPal accounts. Nowadays, the preferred method of payment is via PayPal, as it is a fast, safe and convenient method to pay for services or products, including survey filling.

People who rely on filling surveys online as a source of additional earnings should be aware that not all websites which claim to pay for survey filling actually make such payments. Some companies offer other rewards or points instead, and these rewards or points can only be used for making purchases online. For some people, such rewards or points are a welcome reimbursement for their filling of online questionnaires.

Surveys conducted online are like conversations between companies and customers, and they are conveniently offered not only on websites but are also sent via email. In conformity with the continuously growing number of the social networking sites, surveys are also offered in that space to enable more people to express their opinions online. Online surveys are a great tool that companies have to engage their audiences. They are easy to use, and they can turn into quality content - they can be posted to Facebook pages, or Twitter feeds. Furthermore, companies obtain real-time results, as they can access them immediately after completion.

With the diversity of survey templates available, companies can use the prewritten questions or edit them according to their needs. There are free online tools for creating surveys such as Survey Monkey (http://www.surveymonkey.com), but the better policy is to rely on professional services to create online surveys which can really be effective and instrumental in delivering feedback.

CHAPTER 4

RESPONSIVE WEBSITES

A User-Centered Website

Having a quality website is critical to success in the online world. After all, your website should be at the center of your online presence. If we are to compare your online presence to hosting an event, having a good website is like finding the right location for your event. Despite all of your planning, the success of an event can all come down to location, location, location. The proper venue can make a good event even better, and a bad venue can make an otherwise well-planned event fail. Equally, if no one hears about your event, its unlikely to have good footfall, just like your website.

If you already have a website, you should start by taking a moment and looking at it. As you look at it, ask yourself some key questions. Does my website serve the purpose I originally planned for it? Does it convey what the purpose of my business is? Whom do I want to visit my online business? Am I providing content that those types of visitors want? What is my website really being used for? These are all essential questions to ask yourself about your website to make sure that it is user-centered and effective.

Generally speaking, the result of all of your work on social media, search results, and online ads is to get customers and potential customers to your website. That is because, ideally speaking, your website is where your potential customers can be converted into the real deal and where current customers can find what they are looking for.

If you don't have a website or looking to change it, we encourage you to use the following steps to help your website be exactly what your customers — both current and future — are looking for. However, we also encourage you to make sure that you are not spending all of your budget on a website that nobody can find. Hold some budget back for marketing your site once launched.

Step 1: Have Good Hosting

When it comes to your site running well, hosting makes all the difference. In our opinion, some of the best hosting sites are:

• Fasthosts (We offer our own services via this data centre)

• GoDaddy

• 123-Reg

• Amazon Web Services

You may be wondering, what does a hosting site do? In short, they keep your website up and running, meaning that your site cannot survive and thrive without them. The hosting platforms mentioned above have different strengths and weaknesses. You need to do some research to determine which hosting service is right for you.

Going back to our event analogy; strong hosting for your website is in direct correlation to the environment, location, and resources of a venue. Picking a hosting platform with the right resources for your business will set the stage for your website and business in the digital realm. Using a good venue — i.e. hosting service — makes all the difference for your guests. In a business situation, the hosting platform will take care of essentials like file storage, email hosting, server space, databases and more. They provide these types of resources so that you don't have to provide them yourself. Below we have listed a few key metrics and questions to guide you as you find the right hosting platform for your site.

Basic Metrics to Look For in a Hosting Company:

• An uptime of 99.9% — this means that your website will be up and running on their servers 365 days a year. Anything less can and will be damaging to the business.

• Unmetered/unlimited bandwidth

• Unmetered/unlimited webspace or disc space

• Quality customer service

• High ratings

Additional Questions to Consider:

• How many domains can you have?

• Are you limited on the volume of traffic to your website?

• Do they support e-commerce functionality?

• How much does it cost?

Step 2: Choose an Effective URL

A URL is basically a global address for specific documents, pages, or other resources on the World Wide Web. Put more simply, your URL is what is commonly referred to as your website address, and people use it to locate your site. In fact, the word locater is even in the name: URL stands for Uniform Resource Locator. Facebook's URL is Facebook.com — Following these tips will help you create an effective URL.

Make it Relevant

Your URL should represent either your company name or what visitors will find on your website. It is common practice to use your company name with no spaces followed by a domain name like .com or .co.uk. However, there are times when it makes more sense to have a URL that is related to what you do instead. Either way, your URL should be relevant to your company. If you choose a URL that is not readily associated with your business, you may need to pursue a variety of branding opportunities to connect your web address to your business in people's minds — making your URL relevant to your company. Believe it or not, there was once a time when nobody knew what the URL Google.com was for.

Keep it Short and Simple

There are a lot of good reasons to keep your URL short and simple. Of course, short is relative, but you need to make sure that your URL is short and simple enough to be typed without difficulty. Long and difficult addresses can cause problems for users and introduce opportunities for typos to land people in the wrong place not to mention using them on printed advertising could be tricky.

Things to avoid in your URL:

• Words or names that are difficult to spell

• Excessive and irregular repetition of letters

• Long strings of words

• Hyphens and underscores

When listing your URL on both physical and digital assets, you may choose to capitalise the beginnings of words to help separate them in people's minds. For example, if your URL is something like manywordsstrungtogether.com, you may want to think about listing it as ManyWordsStrungTogether.com*. The capital letters won't affect people's ability to get to your site, but it will help separate the words in their minds.

Make it Effective

Your URL will be present in many different locations. For it to be effective, you'll need to think about how your URL will be used on your social media platforms, on other websites, and even on signs and other physical assets. As mentioned above, you may choose to use capital letters to delineate words within your URL.

Whatever you decide, however, make sure that you are being consistent in your use. To really be effective, it needs to be both clear and memorable. You should also determine if you will want to pursue your URL as a keyword for search results because this will affect how you use your URL on your site and elsewhere.

Keep the User in Mind

In short, you need to keep the user in mind when creating and branding your URL. When your URL is memorable and easy to type, people are more likely to visit your website directly because strong URLs make it easy for users to get to your site.

Some Examples of Strong URLs Are:

• color.adobe.com* – Very simple and highly relevant to the site's content especially since Adobe is already branded in most people's minds.

• www.mashable.com* – Easy to remember and has been branded in the minds of users.

• www.idahofallsfamilydental.com* – This example URL has very strong ties to both an industry — family dentistry — and a location — Idaho Falls — making this a very strong URL.

Some Examples of Weak URLs Are:

• www.manyonline.org — Without strong, targeted branding, most people would not associate this URL with the Museum Association of New York — I found that organisation from that exact search! Interestingly enough, since writing this book the url has now been changed to: www.nysmuseums.org

• www.2sh0rt.com — Using short URLs or confusing characters which are easy to mis-type could lose all meaning without strong, targeted branding.

• www.commoncompanyname.com — Using a common name for your URL gives no indication of what your company is or does, and can become confused with similarly named companies.

Step 3: Build a Strong, Effective Website

As we already mentioned, a strong, effective website should be at the center of your online presence. All of your social media outreach, search engine results and online advertising should be geared toward directing qualified traffic to your site so that you can sell your products or services.

In order to accomplish this, your website needs to be built on a strong foundation — on a strong Content Management System (CMS). Some of the best and most commonly used CMSs are WordPress, Wix and Joomla — although we offer our own unique offering. Finding the right CMS for your website is the key to effectively managing your time while still having a great website. Even if you know how to code, manually coding your website can drain a large amount of time and energy that could be directed more effectively elsewhere in your business.

One of the main benefits of these pre-built CMSs is that they do most of the background coding and programming for you.

If you don't have any web design or coding experience, we would strongly suggest that you have your website designed by a web design company. However, you'll want to make sure that they build your site with a CMS that you can learn how to update yourself. You generally don't want to be responsible for making big changes to your site, but being able to make small updates without working through a third party can be very beneficial under specific circumstances.

Most hosting services will allow you to connect your website directly to your chosen CMS, but it's important to make sure that you can use the two together. The whole point of your CMS is to make website creation easier, not more complicated.

Some additional ways that a good CMS can help you include:

Pre-Designed Themes

A pre-designed theme is essentially a template that can be used with a specific CMS to build a strong, attractive website more quickly. Some of these themes are available for free, but most range in price from £50 to upward of £1000 depending on the developer and the features that are included in the theme. Generally speaking, you get what you pay for so it can be a good idea to invest in a quality theme. ThemeForest,

TemplateMonster and Wix Templates offer many attractive, effective, and mobile-friendly templates that can be used to create a strong website. Many of these themes are also designed to be responsive and look good on a variety of mobile devices as well as in web browsers.

Its worth noting that if you select a popular theme, the chances are that you'll end up seeing a ver similar website, maybe in your industry using the same layout. For this reason, and if budget allows it's a good idea to speak with a web design company who also offers the design and branding services. A uniquely designed website, based purely around your brand and offering will always perform better.

CMS Plugins

Most CMSs offer a variety of plugins that can be used to help you create landing pages, slideshows, and more. Most of the plugins are quick and easy to install, but you may need to take some time to learn exactly how to use the plugins to your advantage.

E-Commerce and Back Office Options

If your website needs to have ecommerce functionality or any other back office options, you'll want to make sure that you choose a CMS that is designed to support these functions. This will allow your website to function correctly without having to spend a lot of time on custom coding. If you are thinking about launching a new website focused on e-commerce then there are a number of dedicated platforms available which may be suitable, these include names such as WooCommerce and Shopify.

Step 4: Create Useful Content

Once you have the right hosting platform, a solid URL, and a strong website to send your users to, it's time to fill it up with content. If we go back to our event analogy, content correlates to the drinks, appetizers, entrées, and desserts that you serve to satisfy your guests once they are at your venue. But you may be asking yourself, what is content? To put it simply, content is information that you present to help your clients and prospective clients. Content comes in a wide variety of forms from on-page text to infographics and videos.

This section is not intended to be a comprehensive look at content marketing, but it should help you understand the basic idea.

Content should be used to strategically funnel your website visitors toward the actions you want them to take. To this end, we suggest creating a variety of content that fits into different sections of what we call the content funnel. Each piece of content should be designed to help your website visitors in some way. The main portions of the content funnel — and the ways you can help your visitors — are to:

• Inform

• Instruct

• Solve

• Sell

Depending on their needs, visitors to your site may enter at different points in this funnel. The best results come when you provide content that addresses their specific needs at the point at which they enter your funnel. Keep in mind, that users are looking for a solution to a problem and you can provide that answer. As with any other strategic funnel, the upper levels are designed to expose a large number of people to your information. The trick is to use upper-level content to help create more qualified traffic to your lower level content. Content can take a wide variety of forms, but it's your job to make sure that it is the relevant solution your users are looking for. And, yes, one piece of content can sometimes fill more than one of these needs.

CHAPTER 5

EMAIL MARKETING

In essence, Email Marketing is a conversation between you and current or prospective customers. It can be used to attract new customers; it can also be used to maintain a relationship with your current customers and business. When writing marketing emails, you have to be very careful of your tone because you don't want to sound like your sole purpose is to make a sales pitch.

In our event analogy, Email Marketing is like sending direct invitations to people who have either attended one of your events in the past or who have expressed interest in your events or events like yours. You would want to send invitations to these people to make sure that they are aware of new events coming up but you would also want to make sure that they aren't just throwing your invitations away.

While Email Marketing may not seem as effective as it was ten or fifteen years ago, it can still be a very relevant to modern digital marketing efforts.

When done correctly, it can be your chance to inform and teach — to build your company and its reputation in the minds of consumers and invite them to create or continue a relationship with you.

Elements of Effective Email Marketing

Inboxes are flooded with new email every day. To be effective, you need to make sure that your emails utilise these elements:

A Strong Subject Line

Your subject line is like a mini ad all by itself. If your subject line doesn't catch a person's attention and, ideally, intrigue them, it is unlikely that they will open and read your email. Take some time to craft your subject line so that it is brief, pointed, and exciting. Make sure that this does not mislead them or comes across as a direct sales message.

Avoidance of Spammy Words

We're all aware of how much email gets filtered out automatically by spam filters. Even if your email makes it past the filters, there are specific words and phrases that a lot of people tend to ignore. Here is a brief list of spammy words to avoid in your marketing email subject lines

- Sale
- Free
- Help
- % Off
- Reminder
- Days of the week

- Donate
- Assistance
- Fwd: and Re:
- Report
- Webinar
- Superlatives like perfect, wonderful, etc

This is by no means a fully comprehensive list, but you get the point. You have to legitimately get a person's attention to have a better shot at having your email opened and read.

Ending with a Call to Action (CTA)

Just like on your website, requesting that people take specific actions can result in them doing so. By ending your email with a CTA, you give them a not so subtle hint of what they should do next. Will everybody perform this action? Probably not. But if you ask people to do something, more of them will than would have if you didn't ask. After all, if you don't ask, the answer is always no.

Personal and Individual

Your emails should be personable and, when appropriate, personalised. People like to feel like they are receiving exclusive information. While most people know intellectually that emails from companies tend to be mass generated, emotionally, they like to feel like they have been singled out to receive this information. Avoid sounding salesy and focus on sounding like a real person who is reaching out to them on an individual basis.

If you decide to personalise the marketing emails you send, make sure that your system is working correctly, and your information is up to date. Personalisation can be harmful to your efforts if you have the wrong data or your system isn't working right because nobody wants to open an email with the wrong name in the subject line or, worse, a placeholder like [NAME].

As you craft your marketing emails, make sure that you keep the reader in mind. Ask yourself questions like what would I want to read? What would get my attention? And how would I feel if this was sent to me?

Effective Email Marketing can be a great source of qualified, interested traffic to your site. Simply put, this is because people who have read and reacted to your emails are more likely to complete conversions on your site.

Lead pages

Lead capture pages is an important marketing tool used by many entrepreneurs and search engine optimisers today. This is considered to be a very sophisticated internet marketing tool used by savvy internet experts while promoting their own business or their clients' business. A lead page can be well defined as a one-page website that acts as marketing tool. This website (lead capture page) is designed to provide excellent information to attract visitors. The main aim of such pages is to arouse the curiosity of the web visitor and inspire them to subscribe or use any of the services of the website.

Lead capture pages need to be made interesting and organised. The primary function of the website is to highlight the various benefits of the website to the visitors. Information is presented in a way so that it highlights the several benefits of the website, its various offers, and other online information which the users can fill-up with interest, in expectation of some benefit. There is also a scope to contact the users directly with the relevant information that might be of interest to them.

There are many characteristics of lead capture pages, such as they usually have a synopsis of information related to their product. Bullet points are often used which explain the benefits of the products. This serves to bring in more and more curious visitors. Internet marketing experts also use autoresponders function so that all queries are immediately attended. The follow-up mail has interesting and compelling data related to different products and services that helps to highlight the usefulness and benefits of the product. It means more and more business in the long run.

There are several ways in which you can use the links in Lead capture pages with any kind of advertising. The links with these pages can be used in flyers, emails, direct mail letters, classified ads, postcards and also business cards. In other words, your lead capture page can be promoted through any of the methods such as pay per click advertising or any advertising that is used by internet marketing experts. You can do these advertisements all by yourself, or you can employ any professional to provide expert services.

Data capture (Opt-Ins, Pop Ups, Subscribe To Download)

Firstly, a brief introduction for those who don't know what it is, data capture is a method of extracting information from forms and surveys that have been filled out by people either by hand or digitally. So, if someone has filled in a survey or form, they can be scanned and captured, and the extracted information used for its original purpose, for research, and using an actual data capture service can save a considerable amount of time doing the work by hand.

That's the basic gist of what data capture is whether for forms, surveys or other documents that need their data extracting and although there has been a standard use for data capture since it was picked up as a useful and popular service.

Besides the advent of the marketing medium itself, no two other things have not only improved upon but also revolutionised email marketing than opt-ins and autoresponders.

Opt-in is nothing more than the little signup form that kindly asks customers to enter their email address and/ or name to receive promotions, deals and general company information in their inbox.

Autoresponders are a bit more complicated than opt-ins, but their impact on email marketing is identical. Autoresponders are scheduled, preplanned emails that share information, updates and deals with customers in their inbox. Autoresponders are a type of email but differ from the email marketing promotions.

In short, opt-ins and autoresponders are completely and utterly integral to email marketing.

Opt-Ins Improves Email Marketing By:

1. Reinforcing Customer Security Online

Of everything that could potentially scare customers online, the number one frightener is losing their identity. If you think about it, we leave a huge and lasting cookie trail (pun intended) across the web with every keystroke and click we make. With the introduction of GDPR in May 2018, the collection, storing and transmission of customer related personal data is as important than ever.

What customers want more than anything from their online experience is control. They want to call the shots, they want to give out their private information when they choose to, and they certainly don't want anyone invading their privacy.

Spammers are avid intruders.

So, opt-in forms are key to providing a sense of security with customers. They're supplying you their email address and allowing you to contact them, when and how they want.

2. Improving Business-to-Customer (B2C) Relationships

Customers are more inclined to trust businesses that offer a chance to sign up. And, what they like even more is the opportunity to get insider information and email-only deals.

Now, with opt-ins, it's customary for businesses to list what the benefits are for signing up in the form itself.

3. Decreasing Chances of Blacklisting

Blacklisting - or labeled a no-good, spammer - is every email marketers' worst nightmare. Essentially, what blacklisting means is that your Internet identity is publicly marked as one that emails without permission (spamming) to loads of unwilling recipients.

However, with the advent of opt-ins, email marketers have dramatically reduced their chances of becoming blacklisted because the power of permission has shifted from the sender to the recipient (customer).

Further, the combination of opt-ins and autoresponders has virtually eliminated the possibility of blacklisting. All of the power is now with the customer rather than the business. Opt-ins have not only revolutionised email marketing but also anything permission-based with other forms of advertising (SMS and fax marketing, namely).

MailChimp

"The best things in life are free" and so is the Mail-Chimp – up to a certain point. MailChimp is the easiest way to create and send professionally functional and aesthetically appealing business emails. It organises and manages subscriptions as well as tracks and evaluates the performance of email marketing campaigns. By using latest analysis techniques like A/B split testing, segmentation and return on investment (ROI) tracking, MailChimp produces the most accurate and instant results out of business email marketing. On top of that, MailChimp is absolutely free to use up to a certain number of subscribers which makes it a unique and mouthwatering service to avail.

But being free only means one thing that MailChimp offers more features and better performance for absolutely nothing compared to those expensive brands and paid marketing service providers.

The secret of MailChimp success as marketer lies in its unlimited features fully updated to be compatible with modern trends and inventions in communication technology. Such features like new subscribers' addition and tracking through mobile make MailChimp as useful on mobile devices as on desktop. Similarly, the social features of MailChimp comprehensively accommodate the rapidly growing people networking sites (Facebook and Twitter) by allowing it to use the power of social networks for business success. This integration is entirely inevitable for a fruitful marketing campaign as it lures heavy crowd by keeping them informed through information sharing. Another essential feature of MailChimp is the integration with third parties (Google Analytics, Eventbrite, WordPress etc.) by enabling smooth data transfer.

The application of MailChimp as an email marketing tool and email list manager is not limited to any particular business or sphere of ecommerce as it has plenty to offer for everyone. This flexibility and array of expert features make MailChimp the most popular and effective email marketing campaigner. The useful tools like Inbox Inspector and Autoresponders ensure prompt access, quality feedback and constant connection with the customers at all times. For email lists organisation and to send targeted promotional messages, MailChimp offers List Segmentation whereas, the Dynamic Content facility allows total customisation of contents based on any criteria set by the client. Other powerful functions like API, RSS to Email and Email Authentication expand the reach of MailChimp beyond the unlimited boundaries of web commerce.

Around half a million satisfied users including small outlets as well as large corporations are the real strength of

MailChimp as the leading email marketing brand and also a proof of its endless success in the ecommerce world.

ConstantContact

Constant Contact offers everything including the gloss as well as the generalities about email marketing services available online. Constant Contact is termed as one of the major players in the email marketing concept, and it has an extensive experience in interactive email marketing on the client level. They have worked with large and diversified clientele including various top-tier brands in the virtual space.

It is the best service that can be hired to send commercial email in response to a specific request, with explicit permission that has been granted to send the email. The service effectively applies email, as an interface to build long term relationships with the customer base. It can also be used to convey massive news and events about the company, to its investors as well as clients.

With constant contact, there is a robust client base that can be trusted with permission email that is authentic and has the potentialities of enhancing the company's sales and revenue margin. Constant contact uses email as a marketing channel and employs some of the best practices that are talked about on the World Wide Web. There are countless benefits available with constant contact email marketing service, as one can send massive news about the company's latest announcements to various organisations whether big or small; thus, maintaining a level of relevant communication with prospects as well as customers.

Using this service, one can build their business effectively and quickly based on using ethical mode of sending massive news to the client base through email. One can also leverage the existing website by using autoresponders. It is handy in writing effective email advertising copy as well as circulating massive news about the progress of the company and can be used to develop newsletters.

Through Constant Contact, many companies have written winning subject lines. It is also possible to put subscription forms on the website. The users can choose to view the email in HTML or text format. Some of the most essential features include a comprehensive feature set included with a template designer to aid in formatting the email campaign for sending massive news through the newsletter facility.

The help center is also available with constant contact, but the only drawback is that they do not offer as many reports as the other email marketing services available on the internet. It also needs to be upgraded for a better integration with the Google Analytics. Today, Constant Contact is touted as the fastest and the most cost-efficient personalised and targeted communication medium available.

CHAPTER 6

COPYWRITING

What Is Copywriting?

Copywriting is defined in the Wikipedia as "the process of writing the words that promote a person, business, opinion, or idea. It may be used as plain text, as a radio or television advertisement, or in a variety of other media. The main purpose of writing this marketing copy, or promotional text, is to persuade the listener or reader to act — to buy a product or subscribe to a certain viewpoint, for instance. Alternatively, a copy might also be intended to dissuade a reader from a par-ticular belief or action."

Copywriting can include body copy, slogans, headlines, direct mail pieces, taglines, jingle lyrics, Internet con-tent, television or radio commercial scripts, press releases, white papers, and other written material incorporated into advertising media. Copywriters can contribute words and ideas to print ads, mail-order catalogs, billboards, commercials, brochures, postcards, online sites, e-mail, letters and other advertising media.

The Art of Copywriting

The art of writing an advertising copy is based on the assumption that words can change the thinking, attitudes, beliefs, and behavior of an audience. If the writings in a copy fail to provoke attention, interest, desire, conviction, and action, it has failed its task and intent.

One of the oldest advertising copywriting formulae is AIDA: Attention, Interest, Desire, and Action. An ad that does not gain the attention of the reader will not to be able to do anything else. Only after catching attention can an ad arouse the interest of the consumer and create the desire for the product, service, or idea presented. Finally, the ad should stimulate some action by the customer. Otherwise, it has failed in its purpose.

Copywriting Techniques

Some techniques a copywriter can use in writing persuasive ad copies include:

• Cliches or buzzwords, such as, now, new, here, at last, and today.

• Action words, such as, buy, try, ask, get, send, taste, watch, look, come, and many more.

• Emotive or exciting words, using adjectives that enhance facts, such as, splendid, surprising, delightful, beautiful, and wonderful.

• Alliteration or a form of repeating sounds pleasing to the ear, but not overdone, obvious, or irritating, such as, 'Let the train take the strain,' 'Don't be vague, ask for Haig,' and 'Go well, go Shell'.

• Colloquialisms or writing to imitate informal speech, such as, 'Pick 'n Choose', 'Fish 'n Chips', and the use of words, such as, don't, wouldn't, won't, what's, and other abbreviations.

• Punctuations and grammar, such as, 'Save the children. Now.' 'Write his name in gold. Remy Martin.'

• Repetition, such as, the use of the same word to open each paragraph, plugging brand or company name throughout the text.

• Intertextuality or the association of a text to other texts or signs, such as the use of the word 'lock' to associate with security, or the use of a statement, term or sign from a movie or other media.

When writing a Headline for a print ad, consider the following guidelines:

• Make the headline a major persuasive component of the ad

• Appeal to the reader's self-interest with a basic promise of benefits

• Inject the maximum information without making it cumbersome or wordy

• Limit headlines to about 5 to 8 words

• Include the brand name in the headline

• Entice the reader to read the body copy

• Entice the reader to examine the visual in the ad

• Never change the typeface in a headline

- Never use a headline whose persuasive impact depends on reading the body copy

- Use simple, common, familiar words

When writing the Subhead, consider the following:

- Subhead should reinforce the headline

- Subhead should entice the reader to proceed to the body copy

- Subheads should stimulate a more complete reading of the entire ad

- The longer the body copy, the more appropriate the use of subheads

- Keep the use of subheads to minimum - they can clutter an ad

When writing the Body Copy, consider the following:

- Use present tense whenever possible

- Use singular nouns and verbs

- Use active verbs

• Use familiar words and phrases

• Vary the length of sentences and paragraphs

• Involve the reader

• Provide support for the unbelievable

• Avoid clichés and superlatives

Some common mistakes to be avoided in copywriting include:

• Vagueness, resulting from the generalisation of words or imprecise meanings.

• Wordiness, where economy of words is paramount because a copy has to fit within limited space and time before it bores the audience.

• Unoriginality, where the use of clichés and worn out superlatives can create a dull and outdated image for a brand or firm.

• Beyond Creativeness, where creativity is taken over-board for the sake of creativity. A copy must remain true to its primary responsibility: communicating the selling message.

CHAPTER 7

SEARCH ENGINE OPTIMISATION (SEO)

If you have looked into digital marketing in recent years, it's possible that you've heard the phrase "SEO is dead." However, nothing could be further from the truth. Search Engine Optimisation has been the lifeblood of being found through search engine searches for well over a decade, and it will continue to be important for years to come. The "dead" part of SEO is attempting to manipulate the signals that search engines use for ranking sites. In recent years, Google and other search engines have caught on to these manipulated signals and worked to minimise the effect of the manipulation and penalise those sites that have used those practices, especially in excess.

Relevant, Useful and Important

In its true form, however, SEO is making sure that your website is following specific, best practices so that Google and other search engines can see and rank your website. Put another way, SEO is creating or improving your website — sometimes in ways that aren't visible — so that the search engines recognise it as being relevant, useful, and important in regards to the question asked by a searcher.

When a search engine thinks that your site is relevant, useful, and important to a search query, it should rank well in the Search Engine Results Pages (SERPs). Unfortunately, SEO is not a "one and done" process. It can be a relatively slow process at the outset and requires consistent effort to maintain. Search engines are constantly evolving, and your SEO strategy has to be able to evolve with them. The power of a good SEO campaign is unbeatable, but it is a very competitive and fast-paced environment.

You should also note that successful rankings and traffic from SEO seldom happen overnight. Instead, you will need to consistently work on your site to make sure that everything is working properly and being seen by search engines. Additionally, you should understand that SEO isn't really about being ranked number one for one specific keyword. In fact, the best SEO strategies target many different keywords and focus on garnering better traffic, not just more traffic for your site. Think about it, would you rather have 1000 visitors with only 10 converting into customers or 100 visitors with 25 converting into customers. Don't get so stuck on rankings, specific keywords, and overall traffic numbers that you lose sight of the overall results that can come from your SEO strategy.

Taking it back to our event analogy, SEO is all of the planning that goes in ahead of time to make sure that the event runs smoothly and that people are aware that the event is happening so that they can attend. For example, if you're hosting a public event, you would want to have the event fully planned and scheduled ahead of time so that there are fewer opportunities for problems to arise. You'd also need to follow applicable deadlines and guidelines to make sure that the local newspapers, magazines, and event listings can publish information about your event in their events calendars so that people who might be interested in your event can hear about it.

Start with a Strategy

Establishing an SEO strategy is like planning your event. The more thought you put into who you want to attend and how you're going to let them know about your event, the more successful you'll be.

Your SEO strategy should begin with these questions:

• Who is your ideal customer?

• Where are they located?

• Where do they spend their time online?

• What words and terms might they use to search for companies like yours?

• What is their likely intent behind each search query?

Optimise Your Website

Once you have a strategy in place, you'll need to optimise your website. Doing so is like following the rules and guidelines established for having your event listed in event calendars and listings. Typically, you can't just call the publisher of an event calendar on the day of your event and expect it to be listed. Similarly, you can't expect SEO to launch you to the top of the search results overnight. Below, we've provided you with some of the most foundational ways in which you should optimise your website to yield long-term SEO results.

1. Utilise Relevant Titles and Meta Descriptions

Your titles and meta descriptions are very important pieces of information because they show up in the search engine results. A page's title is the heading that shows up in the search results, and it is also the name that appears on the tab or window when you are on the page in a web browser. A meta description, on the other hand, is the information that shows up below the title in search results. These two short pieces of information are generally the first impression you get to make on a potential website visitor, so make them count.

Example:

Page: BBC's Homepage (www.bbc.co.uk)

Title: BBC - Home

Meta Description: The best of the BBC, with the latest news and sport headlines, weather, TV & radio highlights and much more from across the whole of BBC On-line.

You should also be aware that search engines can display alternate text from your page if they don't feel that your meta description is relevant to the searcher's query.

2. Submit an Up-To-Date Sitemap

A sitemap is essentially a list of all of the pages on your website. An HTML sitemap is generally accessed via a link in the footer or header of your site and helps visitors find a specific page that may or may not be accessible through your other menus. An XML sitemap, on the other hand, helps Google and other search engines to better crawl and index your site. By submitting an XML sitemap, search engines can discover and index all of the pages on your site more easily. When the search engines can crawl and index new and updated pages on your website and blog, your organic search rankings tend to improve. You can expedite the process of requesting Google to index your pages by logging into your Webmaster Tools account and uploading the xml sitemap, then 'fetching' the url of your html sitemap. By taking this approach, occasionally Google will index your new pages in a matter of hours.

3. Have Relevant Content on Your Pages

As we've already discussed, having relevant content on your pages allows your site to be relevant to searchers' questions. On-page content needs to be written and presented so that it can be used by your site's visitors to answer the questions they have. Search engines exist to help people find what they are looking for on the Internet. It's your job to make sure that the information on your site's pages is relevant to the questions your ideal customers are likely to ask. Don't write for the search engine bots though. If your content isn't useful to real searchers, they are unlikely to stay on your site and become customers.

4. Target Keywords That Are Relevant to Your Business

Your on-page content should include the words and phrases that you want to rank for. If you want people to find your site when they are searching for Blue Widgets, then you'd better have the words Blue Widgets on your site. You should be aware that while ranking for general keywords can be a great goal, it may not be practical due to competition levels and varied searcher intent. Going after less competitive "long tail keywords" can be more productive and result in better-qualified traffic coming to your site. As an example, instead of targeting just the phrase "Blue Widgets," you may want to target a phrase like "Blue Widgets for sale in Your Town"

5. Work to Gain Links from High Ranking Websites

Clear back in the dark ages of the Internet (circa 1997) Larry Page and Sergey Brin wanted to find a better way to organise the seemingly infinite amount of data available on the World Wide Web so that people could find what they were searching for. In the early days of their company — a small endeavor they named Google — they started looking at links between websites as votes approving of those websites. This groundbreaking idea would eventually become the foundation of most modern search engines.

Over nearly two decades, this idea has been refined and become more detailed and complex. Now, instead of simply counting the number of links leading to a specific website, search engines also look at the quality of sites from which those links originate. If the links look "spammy" or are irrelevant to the website they link to, the links will be discounted and the site possibly penalised for low-quality links. Links from a .gov or .edu domain tend to be more trusted than those coming from more general domain types like .com because entities have to prove who they are to get these types of domains. Nevertheless, .com sites that are well established and trusted by the search engines also have more weight when it comes to their links. There are now more than 200 factors which are known to adjust where websites rank in the search results. Each year, Google changes its search algorithm around 500–600 times. While most of these changes are minor, Google occasionally rolls out a "major" algorithmic update (such as Google Panda and Penguin) that affects search results in significant ways.

Mobile Friendly

With the changes in technology over the years, almost every person in the world has a mobile device.

Smartphone sales are increasing by the day, as are tablet sales. This means that more customers are using these devices when searching online than a traditional desktop computer or laptop.

In turn, in order to be a step ahead of your market and reach your audience with ease, you have to have a mobile-friendly website. In addition to appealing to your audience and taking relevant steps to increase your revenue, making your website mobile friendly is also very important to SEO.

The first reason you will find that concentrating on search engine optimisation for your mobile-friendly website is that you will enjoy an increased number of mobile visits. More than seventy-five percent of mobile users will leave a website and search for another if the site isn't mobile friendly, this means that by not taking advantage of this option and not putting together a successful SEO campaign, you could be losing out on valuable business moving forward.

This also improves the user experience. The more users you have visiting your website ensures that the search engines notice and thereby increases your ranking in results. Search engines, such as Google, have put together algorithms that focus purely on mobile-friendly websites. Remember these search engines now focus on user experience rather than keywords and other information, knowing that your customers are enjoying their experience pushes you to the forefront of the pack and helps you increase your ranking and visibility.

Another reason why you will find that making your website mobile friendly is important to SEO is you will notice an increase in revenue. Not paying attention to what Google expects from websites in terms of their mobile users will reduce the chances of you increasing your sales turnover. Bear in mind that more people are using their mobile devices than ever before to search for products and services and make online purchases. To tap into your market and enjoy some of the success, you have to have an SEO friendly mobile website that ticks all of the search engine boxes.

The first and probably most important thing to note is the content. Wording should be easy to read without having to pinch or zoom. There is a significant difference in design between your classic and mobile-friendly website with the mobile-friendly site being quick and easy to read and navigate.

The next thing that you need to do to ensure you tick the boxes is to only use mobile-friendly software, such as Flash. Google is paying close attention to this, and this is what they use to help them identify those mobile-friendly websites and set them apart from those that haven't focused on this sector of the market yet.

The search engine is also paying close attention to whether your customers need to scroll horizontally to read all the information and find what they are looking for. The mobile-friendly website should enable users to easily find what they need without having to navigate scrolls and other things that you would find easy if using a traditional computer mouse while sitting at your desk using your traditional desktop computer.

The final and probably one of the most important things to bear in mind is that your links must be easy to access and easy to tap on using your finger.

All these things combined can determine your success online, bearing in mind that the majority of the younger generation only use mobile over other devices these days.

On Page SEO

On Page SEO is an integral part of Search Engine Optimisation (SEO) activities. Before answering the question "What Is On Page SEO?" it is useful to look at some of the factors that are considered by the search engines when deciding how to rank a page or post.

These are:

Off Page Factors - This grouping relates to backlinks to a site and carries the highest weighting in determining ranking. Factors evaluated include how many backlinks exist, the authority of the linking sites, the anchor text of the links and how relevant the linking content is. This is other sites voting for your page and telling the search engines that your page is relevant to the searched keyword.

Other factors - These are various factors most of which are not directly under the control of the webmaster. Included are things like how busy the site is (traffic), how old the domain is and how fast the page loads.

On Page Factors - Search engines regularly send their "spiders" to index pages on the web. As part of this process, they log the terms to which each page is relevant. Of course, these "spiders" cannot understand the content, so it is vital that the page is laid out in such a way that there is no confusion. If the search engines are unclear as to the relevancy of a page, it will be tough to get a high ranking. The answer to "What is On-Page SEO?" is that it is the means by which the webmaster ensures that the search engines are clear as to the relevancy of the page.

It is important to remember that although on page SEO may be allocated a lower weighting than the other two groups in deciding ranking, it is still a vital part of overall SEO activities. If it is not done properly a high ranking will be very hard to achieve even with many backlinks.

As On page SEO is fully under the webmaster's control it is the easiest part to get right, and there is really no excuse for not doing so.

On Page SEO is essentially structuring the site in a way that is search engine friendly. Each page or post should be built around a keyword so that it is clear to the search engines that it is highly relevant to that keyword. At the same time, it is essential that the content should still be good for human visitors.

What this means is that you have to get used to writing a way that is SEO friendly. This has been described as writing for an adult audience but so that a 6-year-old could at least understand the subject. This takes some practice, and you really need to go through a detailed checklist before publishing to make sure your on-page SEO is correct.

CHAPTER 8

SOCIAL MEDIA

What is Social Media?

Social Media is a platform that lets us participate in social networking. We can share our posts on various social media platforms to improve personal and business visibility. Today it is the best source for news updates, marketing, education, and entertainment.

Business in today's day and age is dominated by customers and their demands. People prefer to see referrals, reviews over Google search results, or a website before purchasing a product. To stand by the flow, we need to learn what people say about us. You need to actively participate in relevant communities to interact and influence masses. You need to engage with social media to manage your online reputation.

Social media marketing is a must to target a wider customer base and expand your business. Social Media

Marketing is the activity of driving website traffic through social media sites.

Facebook Marketing

Facebook is a social networking service provider. It lets you invite and connect with friends, send messages and pictures, like and comment or share them. Facebook has seen outstanding growth since its inception and is poised to maintain its dominance in social networking.

History of Facebook

Harvard student, Mark Zuckerberg founded Facebook on February 4, 2004. In May 2007, Facebook opened up its developer platform to allow third-party developers to build applications and widgets that, once approved, could be distributed through the Facebook community. In May 2008, Facebook engineers announced Facebook Connect, a cross-site initiative that allows users to publish on third-party sites in their Facebook newsfeed. The site was redesigned in late 2008, intended to streamline the website and make it easier to see what friends were doing.

What is Facebook Marketing?

Facebook is undoubtedly the most popular social media platform available with many advantages associated with it. It is primarily a social networking site; however, it can be used as a handy tool for promoting and advertising a business. We can use Facebook to promote a brand, market a company, or create awareness about a service or a product.

Success with this form of marketing requires more than a fan page and a few friends. When used effectively, Facebook marketing can provide a business with exciting benefits and results. Facebook marketing can enable businesspeople to significantly improve their brand awareness and reach out to a wider audience.

Twitter Marketing

Twitter is another social networking platform that allows registered users to read and write 140-character (moving to 280 as a trial to a group of users) messages called 'tweets.' It is available on all devices such as cell phones, desktops, laptops, and tablets.

History of Twitter

Jack Dorsey, an undergraduate student at New York University, introduced the idea of an individual using a message service to communicate with a small group. Twitter was launched as an SMS-based communication platform. Initially, it was known as "twttr." On March 21, 2006, Jack Dorsey sent the first ever tweet: "just setting up my twttr."

What is Twitter Marketing?

Twitter marketing is a powerful tool for companies of every size and structure to reach out to new customers, promote their brand, and connect with the rest of the companies. Users can find out if customers are talking about them, and the business can accordingly respond. Tweets create another instance for the business that shows up in the search engine results such as Google. Twitter serves as a solid foundation for your business to branch out into other social sites.

Twitter is a great platform for projecting what your company is doing in real-time and accessing a large audience, where your Tweets can promote products and events.

Linkedin Marketing

LinkedIn is a business-oriented social networking site launched in 2003. It has 740+ million users across the world. It is available in 20 languages. It allows users to create and customise profiles and connect with people having similar interest areas.

Presently, it is the largest platform for social networking, assisting people with job opportunities. Job seekers can connect and follow hiring managers and can update their profiles in a defined fashion to get easily discovered.

One can follow a company, get notifications, bookmark jobs, like and comment other's posts, and invite others on LinkedIn. The best part of LinkedIn is that you can see your recent visitors and endorse others' skills.

History of LinkedIn

LinkedIn was founded in 2002 by Reid Hoffman, and it was launched in 2003. Early on, its growth was slow, but it accelerated by the end of 2003.

• In 2004, it introduced new features such as the ability to upload addresses to invite others and introduce groups and partners with American Express. It assorted 1 million members.

• Jobs and subscriptions were introduced in 2005. Membership toll increased to 4M.

• In 2006, LinkedIn launched public profiles as your current and past career record.

• In 2007, Reid Hoffman stepped aside, and Dan Nye took over. Membership toll rises to 17 M.

• In 2008, LinkedIn became global by opening its office in London and launching the Spanish and French version of the website.

• In 2009, the membership count tipped over 50 million. Jeff Weiner joined LinkedIn as its CEO.

• In 2010, LinkedIn grew amazingly with 90 million members and 1000 employees in 10 offices around the globe.

• In 2011, LinkedIn became a publicly traded company on New York Stock Exchange and hosted a Town Hall meeting with Obama. Membership reaches 135 million.

• The site was redesigned in 2012 focusing on making LinkedIn simpler and easy to use.

• LinkedIn turned ten in 2013 with 225 million users across the globe.

• By the end of 2014, Linkedin had grown to a significant extent with 315+ million registered users and well over 5000 employees in 27 cities. It continues to grow, adding features and delivering its users a better experience every time they log onto LinkedIn.

LinkedIn Marketing

LinkedIn is a professional networking platform, and it has all the features of a great marketing opportunity provider. Here you interact with people who mean business. To market through LinkedIn, you need to do the following:

• Build a robust business page that displays your products and services in a compelling format.

• Invite clients and vendors to follow and recommend your page.

• Launch a group that is related to your business. It can attract significant traffic.

• Reach your audience through targeted advertising.

LinkedIn is a powerful social media tool. You just need to follow its policies and best practices.

Youtube Marketing

YouTube is an online video hosting service that lets people share their videos. Businesses and individuals use YouTube to share or find videos, including entertainment, promotions and instructions.

YouTube is the most popular video hosting service, followed by similar services such as Vimeo, Facebook video and Flickr. Like other social media channels, You-

Tube enables people around the world to interact, share and create content through online communities.

Because of its popularity and features, YouTube can be a useful marketing channel for businesses. Your business could use YouTube to launch or promote products, express your brand's 'personality', monitor feedback, provide customer service and help your customers spread the word about your business.

How YouTube works

YouTube began in early 2005 and has grown rapidly. Every minute, people around the world upload more than 300 hours worth of video footage to YouTube.

YouTube has the second-largest search engine in the world, behind Google (which owns YouTube). This means people are constantly searching for information using YouTube and discovering videos relating to these topics.

Google+ Marketing

June 2011 saw the beginning of a limited field trial of Google Plus. Google, the owner of the most popular search engine on the web, is taking on Facebook and Twitter to get its piece of the social networking pie. Even with the limited trial, Google+ already has over 10 million users within several weeks. Here are some of the benefits of Google+ and more information about the Google+ Project.

Google+ One: Google introduced Google+ One on June 1, 2011. It is similar to the Facebook Like button and is an icon with +1 inside of it. The button can be placed on any page of a website and will signify that the content is important and recommended by other people. Information about clicks on the button will be used in the search results algorithm and will help to increase search rankings. Google itself claims that the +1 will not only increase traffic to a site but that traffic will be higher quality. Adding this button to your website is as easy as visiting the Google website. There you will choose one of the four sizes available and one of the 40 languages.

Circles: Circles is a feature that allows you to group your contacts. The main Google+ Benefit of this feature is that there may be information that you don't want to share with everybody. Circles may include friends, family, friends from work, acquaintances, relatives, etc. This Google+ Feature is easier to use than Facebook groups. All you do is drag the contact and place him or her into the circle.

Hangouts and Huddles: A hangout is a place to video chat with your friends on one screen. An awesome Google+ Benefit is that up to ten people can use this function via webcam. You click on the Welcome button and choose contacts or circles. A huddle puts people together for a group chat on your mobile device. These have been shown to be very popular features of Google Plus.

Sparks: Sparks is a way to share articles, pictures, and videos with friends and family. When you click on the Share button, you will be able to choose which circles or individuals to share the content with. Also, sparks will present a drop-down menu that will predict your topic when you search, similar to the old Google search. The dashboard will contain subjects you search for so you can access them easily.

Privacy: The privacy features of Google+ are similar to Facebook but superior to Twitter. Privacy is a major benefit because you share content only with the people you choose. Also, no person is added to a circle without your consent. There is an added feature that will stop contacts from sharing your content with someone else. You also have the ability to edit a post after posting it, and you decide if you will allow comments.

Vimeo Vs YouTube Marketing

As a small business owner, you have to get your message across to your audience quickly and efficiently. Posting videos is one of the best ways to spread your message, and for this, it is better to go for a single video platform so that your audience doesn't get confused.

You have two options; YouTube and Vimeo. YouTube has a huge audience base but low video resolution while Vimeo has a relatively smaller audience base and higher video resolution. So, which platform should you post your videos on? You can make this decision based on the following criteria.

Quality

YouTube:

According to statistics, about 1 billion people visit You-Tube on a regular basis, and about 170 million people visit Vimeo on a regular basis. YouTube has a large number of audiences for small business to present their products or service.

YouTube is free to use, and anyone with a Google account can upload their videos on the site making the competition more intense. Moreover, YouTube takes money from advertisers to show their business videos before the actual video is played. For your business, it can be a disadvantage because your competitors' video may get played before your own.

Advantage: YouTube is an ideal video platform having tons of users with diverse needs.

Vimeo:

As far as popularity goes, Vimeo is behind YouTube but is more user-friendly. Besides, Vimeo contributors are higher quality and post more informative content. Since business accounts are not free on Vimeo, each company or business posts highest quality videos on Vimeo.

With respect to speed and technical quality of videos, both YouTube and Vimeo go side by side. Both the platforms allow you to play 1080p videos at 4k speed. But Vimeo offers another feature. It lets you know how many times a video is played and if the users finished watching the whole video.

Advantage: Vimeo offers relatively higher quality videos with more accurate statistics.

Reach

YouTube:

If your audience is not familiar with your product or service, Vimeo can help since it is more business centered and gives a direct connection to your site. On the other hand, YouTube keeps visitors on its platform which can reduce the number of visitors to your site.

However, YouTube has an upside: it offers a much better search function, which returns a variety of videos on the basis of the keyword entered. On the other hand, Vimeo has to be more specific.

Since Google owns YouTube, users will get more results from YouTube than from Vimeo for a given search term.

Advantage: It's easier for users to search for a specific YouTube video on Google.

Vimeo:

Since anyone can use YouTube, the platform doesn't have a structured community, unlike Vimeo. YouTube offers three privacy options, but Vimeo offers six to satisfy your business needs.

Advantage: Vimeo has better classification into groups of users making it easier for you to get your message across to potential customers.

Benefits for Business

YouTube:

YouTube offers following significant benefits for business users:

· More traffic from Google

· Comments from users

· Free of cost hosting

· Advertising offers

· Huge audience

· HD videos with fast speed

Vimeo:

The advantages of Vimeo for businesses are:

· A controlled community

· Better statistics

· Smaller, professional audience

· Customer service support

· HD videos with fast speed

Instagram Marketing

Millions of people globally are now using Instagram. Instagram has made it easier to take pictures and share them with friends, and many people enjoy doing this. Apart from networking, you can use Instagram in a more efficient way for marketing. Instagram is a great promotional tool you can use to promote your business online.

Tell the story using photos and videos. Photos are worth a thousand words and Instagram is all about pictures. If you are into Instagram for marketing purposes, then you ought to understand that random photos do not work. You need to post pictures of your product constantly. Posting pictures of your products is one of the best ways of increasing your brand awareness and boost sales of your products. The pictures do not necessarily need to be very professional. The key thing is having the pictures highlight the main features and functions of the goods you are promoting. The pictures should appeal to a vast audience on Instagram.

Videos too are important in Instagram marketing. You can create and share a video with your employees to promote the product at hand. As with Facebook and

LinkedIn you could also opt to do a live product review video and share it on Instagram. Pictures and videos are more appealing to many people than plain text posts. Media files stand higher chances of going viral as people share them. They are also more memorable than just text. Create photos and videos that show your brand story and values. So, images and videos are important if you want to improve your brand and sales.

Use quality media

To improve your visibility, you need to make and share high-quality photos and videos in your feeds. Where necessary, seek professional assistance or advice from a photographer. However, you can use a great camera to take sharp pictures – most recent mobile phones are more than capable of taking high quality photos and in most cases HD videos. Try to get your images at best angles. Edit your photos for better results. Nowadays mobile phones are also equipped with photo editing tools for this purpose. Instagram too has several photo editing tools. Apply this tools for your Instagram marketing purpose.

Connect with our followers

Maintaining contact with your customers is vital, particularly for developing business with a small market share. You can start by showing your clients that you are concerned about their feedback. You can achieve this by replying to their questions and comments. This will improve user-generated content and credibility as well as promote the visibility of your products and business. Your Instagram followers can significantly influence the success of your enterprise, and you should never underestimate them.

Use hashtags

Like the majority of the social platforms, hashtags are relevant in Instagram marketing too. You need to use them because Instagram users interact using hashtags. Hashtags allow users to make your contents searchable and are important if you want to increase your followers. Has tags like media can create a viral effect which is beneficial to your business. You can also take advantage of trending hashtags especially if the hashtags are related to your product. This is important because Instagram users can use hashtags to search for posts.

Use branded hashtag

You should include your business name in your hashtags. Use unique hashtags for a particular promotional campaign you run. Not only does this promote your campaign, but it also provides a unique hashtag for your clients to connect and share with other participants.

Have a friendly attitude to everyone

While carrying out your Instagram marketing, you need to understand that Instagram is a community composed of people with varied ideas, emotions, and background. Always be friendly to everyone and appreciate their time to connect with you on your page. Always ensure you listen to your clients.

Be active

Post at least once daily to keep things up to date to ensure your followers are updated with the current happenings. You can experiment posting at varying times of the day to see which time your posts do best.

Consistency

Consistency is crucial in Instagram marketing. Be consistent with your postings and develop a theme that is prominent in your posts. Let your followers know what to expect from you.

Connect your Instagram and Facebook accounts to improve your marketing power. Nowadays, you can have an Instagram tab on your Facebook page. This allows you to share your Instagram posts to your Facebook followers if you have a fan page.

You can network with friends and the world via Instagram. Instagram can be used for marketing purposes. Instagram marketing can improve your brand's visibility, increase sales, and consequently revenues. Consider the above-mentioned Instagram marketing tips to achieve success.

Pinterest Marketing

Pinterest is a pinboard-style, social sharing site where people can pin photos, graphic images, infographics and videos. Although many people initially thought of Pinterest as a place to share images reflecting personal hobbies and interests, the impact on business success when promoting through Pinterest cannot be ignored.

In fact, Public Relations, SEO & Marketing, Graphics, and Venture Capitalism rank among Pinterest users' top 10 interests.

Started 9 years ago (December 2009), Pinterest already boasts over 70 million users, 72% of which are women who love to spend money and have the money to do so. Pinterest has shouldered its way between Facebook (20% of Facebook users are on Pinterest every day) and Twitter and is now considered one of the top social media referral source for ecommerce based business websites.

Pinterest drives more referral traffic than YouTube, LinkedIn and Google+ put together. And traffic arriving to websites from Pinterest is found to be 10% more likely to buy and spend on average 10% more than visitors arriving from other social media sites.

Only a handful of Pinterest notable influencers are top-selling retailers and magazines - the majority are bloggers, individuals and small businesses. It's time to start taking this site very seriously.

So how do you set up an optimised business account, get followers and drive traffic to your websites through pinning? Here are 5 Tips to get you started:

Tip #1: Open a Pinterest Business account - it's free — make sure you optimise it by using your business name and keywords on your Pinterest home page. When you start your business page, you will be asked to create a username; this is your first opportunity to brand your business on Pinterest.

You don't have to use your business name if using a focus keyword or keyword phrase would suit your marketing purposes better.

Tip #2: Create targeted pin boards - keep in mind target market, and different aspects of your brand, don't be afraid to add personal interests. Your prospects and customers are buying from YOU, not just your brand. You are more likely to attract followers if you mix it up.

Tip #3: Make your website pinnable - ensure that you have plenty of pictures and video on your site for pinning by you and others as well. Add a 'Pin-It' button to your site to make it easy for visitors to pin to their boards - again adding to your viral reach.

Tip #4: Link your photos and videos back to your website. After you have posted an image or video to your board, re-open it and put your website or web page URL where you want to drive traffic. This is an important step in getting Pinterest traffic to go to your website.

Once you do this, every time one of your pins get 'liked' or re-pinned, you are increasing the likelihood that it will result in you getting a referral to your website.

Tip #5: Spend time engaging with other people's boards - it's just like any other social media site - you have to 'pay to play.' Meaning, if you want others to engage and re-pin your pins, you have to spend some time doing the same.

As with all online marketing activities, you should check your analytics to ensure your efforts are getting results -

This allows you to track how many people have been pinning from your website and how many people have viewed your pins. Make adjustments based on your findings.

CHAPTER 9

PAID/PER PER CLICK ADVERTISING

Google AdWords

Everyone wants to be a 'Google AdWord professional' and who wouldn't? The Google advertising team has given any and every inspiring Internet marketer an open gateway to make money with AdWord advertising. Using AdWords can lead to much success as a marketer.

Google PPC

Google PPC may be one of the easiest ways to generate traffic to your website and make some decent profits from your AdWords campaign. Google AdWords is the most popular form of pay per click advertising for small businesses, partly because of Google and their AdWord advertising popularity, and partly because it allows you to control your expenses by setting daily maximums for each ad in your Google AdWord campaign. In your

Google AdWord campaign, you set how much you are willing to invest in PPC (pay per click) and how much your daily budget is. These numbers in your Google AdWord campaign determine how often your actual ad will show on a viewer's screen when she hits the search button. Advertisers who have set their AdWord Campaign budget highest, and are bidding higher on that particular keyword, shows up first in Google's Sponsored results.

Google AdWords advertising usually starts off as a trial and error for marketers who are new to using AdWords. It comes down to you having to spend some to make some. And often times, you are going to find yourself losing a lot more than you're making. It's going to take a lot of reading and research to learn Google AdWords, how it works, and how to become profitable from it. An AdWord campaign is more than guessing and throwing numbers together. To become a Google AdWords professional, you MUST study your niche, choose your AdWord keyword list wisely, and refrain from any bidding wars. Bid on what you feel comfortable with. Once you start making more money from your Google Ad-

Word campaign, then you can slowly start upping your bids, but NOT right away.

AdWords Campaign

Google AdWords allows you to run numerous AdWords campaigns at the same time. This is key. Most would suggest starting with the "Search Network Only" option, but you can change this as you learn and grow. It's a good idea to start with a naming system that you will keep using, so you don't get confused somewhere down the line. For each campaign you can designate geographic area targets, budgets and group your Ads together.

Make Money Using AdWords

Now you should already know how Google AdWords can be a great thing; now we'll show how to use it for your business to make profit. First, you should determine how much you can afford to pay for a click. Doing this is important because it enables you to understand the amount of money you can bid on keywords in your Google AdWord campaign while still remaining profitable. To do this your conversion ratio is needed, calculate your conversion ratio by dividing your monthly unique visitors by your monthly sales, then convert your answer into a percentage by multiplying by 100.

Imagine in a month you get 20000 visitors and sell 500 products each with a gross profit for you of £50. Your conversion ratio simply put is (500/20000) *100 = 2.5%. This means that for every 100 people who visit your site 2.5 buy your product.

Your gross profit per 100 visitors is calculated by multiply the gross profit on your product by your conversion ratio, to continue with the previous example - £50 x 2.5 – £125. Divide your gross profit per 100 visitors figure by 100 to determine how much you can bid in your Google AdWord campaign.

In this case, you could afford to pay up to £1.25 in AdWord adverting for a visitor and still break even. You probably will not be paying this much for a click; the minimum CPC on Google AdWords is only a few pence so play your cards right and you can have high profits.

Bing Ads

Bing Ads is awesome too. They aren't as large as Google AdWords - but it's a combination of Bing and Yahoo. So, you can still get mega traffic from this program. And guess what? Although there are a lot of people who use Bing Ads... you won't have as much competition as you would with Google AdWords.

Bing has become one of the most used search engines on the web alongside Google over the last few years. Known as the "decision engine," it has generated a new precise search option for users. Bing search has some stand out features that make it such a popular choice for people in need of any kind of information, these include listing of search suggestions, video thumbnails for previewing and instant answers for sports, finance and consumer needs. Bing has grown to be the 3rd most highly used search engine on the internet and continues to make minor adjustments which has only enhanced its popularity.

Using Bing will allow you access to some great options while drastically improving your search time. Bing search offers instant answers for most of your needs. For sports, Bing search offers the most up to date scores, stats and news displayed daily so you can stay connected to your favorite teams. This is also utilised with finance as well. For those who are constantly checking their stocks, Bing search allows easy access to live stock quotes by just adding the symbol of the company in the search box. This is one of the most popular features Bing search provides because it eliminates a lot of time for the user.

Bing search also offers a preview thumbnail of videos and news clips for the user's enjoyment. This makes deciding on what to click on simpler. Other media features that are included in Bing search is the use of image search and video search. These allow for more precise searches over the internet making it easier to find exactly what you are looking for as well as other suggestions that you may enjoy. Bing is a powerful search engine dedicated to helping you find what you are looking for promptly.

One of the most notable features that Bing offers is their search suggestions. Search suggestions allow Bing to assist you in finding exactly what you need by providing alternative options that may help you as well. This feature is provided in the form of a list that is displayed on the side panel for easy access. This feature is what triggered the name "decision engine" because it provides numerous related options for the user to click and view. Using Bing search is a great way for you to locate information, products, services, businesses and entertainment in the click of a button.

With Bing, you will have access to as much information you can ever handle. These are just a few of the top features that are provided, but Bing also offers local solutions with up to date traffic, weather and local entertainment information. Bing search makes it easy for you to find the best restaurants, movie theatres, nightclubs and bars in your city. The integration with Hotmail makes finding precise information like restaurant reviews and movie reviews simple and easy. Using Bing is an excellent way for you to stay connected to the world of news and entertainment without ever leaving your home.

Remarketing

Remarketing is a feature in Google AdWords tool that allows you to revisit or follow people who have previously visited your site or have shown interest in your products. It is a technique of leaving a lasting impression in the mind of a visitor by showing them relevant ads across the web. Another term for remarketing is 'retargeting'. This feature helps you remind your prospective buyers about your products and services.

How Does Remarketing Work?

Using the remarketing feature for your website is simple, and you need to follow a few simple steps to achieve optimum results. First of all, you need to add the piece of code given by AdWords, known as the remarketing tag, to all your site pages. The code can be added anywhere; however, ideally, it should be added to either the header or the footer. Once it is done, you can create remarketing lists for any of your webpages. When someone visits the page, their cookie ID is added to the list, and your ad keeps following them until they clear his cookies. You can go ahead and create a campaign in AdWords to target specific types of audiences. You can create separate campaigns for targeting varied visitors also.

Why would you use remarketing?

Remarketing is a convenient and advanced way of targeting a specific category of audience that you think can become future customers of your products. The best way to ensure maximum return on investment is to target the right audience and show them relevant ads, more than once. This would not only leave a mark in their minds but would also remind them to check out your products once they are ready to make a purchase. In short, remarketing is one of the most apt tools for customer engagement and is known to improve conversions radically.

What are the different types of remarketing?

There are many types of remarketing through which you can target your audience. You can remarket through the display network, search ads, dynamic remarketing for advertisers with a Google merchant center account, and for mobile apps.

How to select your target audience?

There are various kinds of people searching for innumerable things on the Internet. The first step to achieving success in remarketing is to decide your audience. Before developing a strategy, you need to collate your data and analyse it. You will then have to decide upon a specific group of people whom you would like to target. This group/s should ideally be of those people who are your prospective customers. You can have various parameters to decide upon your target audience. For example, the pages that they visited, number of visits, time spent on particular product pages, etc.

Who should use remarketing?

Remarketing is a strategy that is useful for every website that wishes to improve its sales, promote brand awareness, or better audience loyalty. It is a valuable tool that can improve ROI for any business.

Benefits of remarketing with Google

The most important benefit of remarketing with Google is that your prospective customer will think of your brand/products when he/she decides to make a purchase. You can also improve and customise your strategies according to the needs and requirements of your customers. You can reach out to a large number of people and target various sets of audience in different ways. You can also use your creativity to make different kinds of ads to target the same or different groups of people. Through bids, you can decide which sites to show your ads on, and therefore, get maximum ROI through efficient pricing.

CHAPTER 10

TRACKING & ANALYSIS

Google Analytics

Google Analytics is a free enterprise-class web analytics solution offered free by Google. Google Analytics generates detailed statistics about the visitors and web traffic generated for a website. Using Google Analytics with your website is an excellent idea because it takes minutes to sign up for and will provide you all the necessary metrics you'll need to determine what is working, or not working, on your website for successfully capturing new sales for your business.

Its intuitive user interface provides you easy access to all data, allowing you to obtain the key information you need for your website quickly. Google Analytics keeps track of how all visitors found your website including exact keyword searches from different search engines and which other websites linking to you referred visitors to you. Google Analytics allows you to track the effectiveness of your marketing programs, email marketing, pay per click networks, unpaid organic search, and much more.

Google Analytics is also integrated with Google AdWords. Google AdWords will display an ad for your business on Google search results pages and their advertising network on a pay per click basis; that is, you only pay Google an advertising fee if people click your ads directing them to your website.

Using Google Analytics in conjunction with Google AdWords optimises your online marketing campaigns by tracking your sites landing page quality and conversion goals. By using Google Analytics, you can determine which ads are performing well, and which are not, providing the information to minimise or select appropriate keywords for AdWords campaigns.

The following are 10 essential features of Google Analytics:

1. Google Analytics allows you to compare data about the performance of your site at two different time periods. It also allows you to chart the data im-

mediately to get a better view of your site. It shows you the performance of your site based on area, city or country metrics.

2. Providing referring sites and search results metrics are the basic features of any analytics program, but with Google Analytics you can get statistics not only on the number of visitors a link partner is sending but the quality of the traffic.

3. Once you have your business goals, for example, sales & marketing, set up in Google Analytics, you can determine and thus control vast amounts of data with regard to what's working and what's not in your marketing strategy.

4. Google Analytics allows complete AdWords integration. This means it provides data on each group, campaign, and keyword. Specifically, you can look at each of these areas and see the number of displays, clicks, your cost, conversion, etc.

5. It enables you to customise the rich features provided in your Google Analytics dashboard. You can

move the most often used reports to the dashboard for fast access by just clicking the "Add to Dashboard" link.

6. The Google Analytics dashboard feature allows you to schedule and automatically send recurring email updates to yourself or other recipients within your business using multiple formats.

7. Google Analytics shows you the popularity and effectiveness of each link on every page of your site. These powerful and graphical reports display the effectiveness of your site design in a visual model.

8. Google Analytics navigation summary report shows where your users go from the homepage, or how most of them get to your contact page. If people aren't following your desired navigation, it means you probably need to correct some things on your page to compel users to click on the areas you desire.

9. Google Analytics tells you what search keywords people are using to find your site. If certain keywords are proving hot, you might want to consider focusing a Google AdWords campaign using these keywords and content. It also tells you how your customers find you.

10. The search engine traffic metric illustrates which search engines are sending the most traffic to your website and how well it's converting into sales. This will help you optimise your marketing spend and SEO efforts.

In addition to the 10 reasons mentioned above, Google Analytics also has a "Report Finder" to help you search for your archived reports, helps you view your website's bounce rate over time, shows connection speed data which helps you determine how to prioritise and optimise your site's design and load time, and much more.

To start using Google Analytics navigate to http://www.google.com/analytics/. You can either register using your existing Google account, for example, if you already have a Gmail account or sign up for a new one. Google Analytics is a feature-rich, free application that every website owner should consider integrating into their site.

Developing a website is one thing - after that what is also needed, is to monitor its efficacy and that of your digital marketing, whether it is worth the money that is being spent. You should study the type of visitors that your website is getting and the business that is being generated. This will help you in determining as to what changes will be needed to prevent a downward trend. One can hopefully generate more internet traffic by the various digital marketing strategies outlined previously.

Visitor Tracking

User attention spans are getting shorter. You'll have just 3-7 seconds on average to capture a visitor's attention. With such a short amount of time to get your message across, you firstly need to ensure you have a well optimised website that immediately shows what products and services are being offered and what value they offer to the potential customer.

But even if your can move your visitors into the various product and service pages, how can you ensure they use your call to actions, fill out your forms or connect to you on social media? You simply can't.

This is where Visitor Tracking really helps.

Imagine if you could not only highlight your visitors but convert ready-to-buy prospects, before your competitors even get close?

Visitor Tracking software is the software that reveals the identity of your anonymous website traffic, and turns them into actionable sales leads. In real-time.

Much like Google Analytics, the Visitor Tracking software uses a small piece of code which is inserted on your website pages which tracks IP addresses visiting a website. Those IP addresses are then matched to data held by online databases and in-turn then provides accurate information about these website visitors. This information can generally include the company name, address and website information. On occasions this could also include key points of contact and their social media channels.

Furthermore, by using this essential contact information to reach out to the visitor, you can deliver a tailored offering based on the pages and content the visitor has looked at.

You can sign-up for this software with companies such as LeadForensics, a market leader or via our own platform by visiting the following url: https://www.123internet.agency/strategy/

Dashboards

Although traditional management reporting has been around for decades, it is quickly becoming out of date. Let's face it, who wants to wait for "stale" reports from managers when technology now enables us to have up-to-the-minute information at our fingertips in the form of a business dashboard? Like the dashboard in your car, a business dashboard places real-time knowledge in front of executives, managers and teams to help them drive the operations under their responsibility. Dashboards can help companies put fires out while they are small and capture opportunities the moment they arise. Whether your organisation is planning to develop business dashboards or even if it already has dashboards in place, here are 5 important ways to get the most out of them:

1. Include Only Actionable Measurements

Since the core purpose of a dashboard is to support decision-making, only actionable information should be included. For example, it may be nice to know the number of employees in a certain department, but whether or not payroll expense is in line with the plan is actionable. Financial and operational key performance indicators, or "KPIs", are especially appropriate to include in business dashboards because they highlight how the company is doing in the areas that matter most.

2. Design A System For Information Flow

Whenever possible, business dashboards should not be separately contrived or maintained by specific people. Humans make mistakes, they go on vacation, have competing priorities and will ultimately tire of constantly searching for data and entering it on a dashboard for managers. Instead, it is always best if dashboards are automatically fed with information flowing from documents and files that teams normally use to run their operations. For organisations where large amounts of disparate, raw data is generated across many departments, a business intelligence system can be used to turn the data into important insights on a dashboard.

3. Include All Teams

Business dashboards are not just for managers and executives. On the contrary, every team in the company should have its own dashboard that tracks its financial and operational results. Likewise, each person should be aware of how their team is performing, and regular meetings or huddles should focus on the team's dashboard and underlying data. Just as team dashboards flow from the documents that are used in their operations, management and executive dashboards can in turn flow from team dashboards.

4. Make Information Simple and Visually Clear

By their nature, one quick look at a dashboard should be all it takes to understand how a company or team is doing. When the information is too complicated, a dashboard quickly loses effectiveness. Also, it is important not to go wild with graphs and charts. Graphical displays can often be quite powerful, but sometimes dashboards can be so full of graphs and charts that the page becomes convoluted and distractive.

5. Allow "Drill Down" To Underlying Data

When questions arise from a business dashboard, it's inconvenient to have to call someone or send out an e-mail asking for an explanation or additional information. Instead, clicking on a dashboard amount to display the underlying data can answer questions immediately. Of course, not every company has the time and funds to develop a comprehensive data system that supports their dashboard, but it is a worthy goal to connect dashboards with as many supporting details as possible.

When thoughtfully implemented, business dashboards can make a big difference in organisational success, especially when they are cascaded across the company and used for decision-making by every team. As competitiveness continues to increase the need for clear, easily accessible, real-time information, we will wonder what we ever did without our dashboards!

Utilise A Dashboard For Your Marketing Results

With the vast array of digital marketing activities, creating and monitoring a dashboard which consolidates this information into simply actionable metrics is a huge step to ensuring your marketing strategy is a success.

 We have already learned about the various social media platforms and the data which can be accessed via Google Analytics. The next step is to pool this data via APIs into a single, graphical dashboard. Luckily there are providers who can supply this software for you, much like our own dashboard which was developed specifically to monitor digital marketing activities.

You can access this dashboard by simply visiting:

https://www.123internet.agency/strategy/reporting-dashboard/

CONCLUSION

Every business is different. Therefore, every business must approach their digital marketing with a unique plan. Because everybody's path to success will be different, we didn't set out to provide a step-by-step guide to online success. As mentioned earlier in the introduction to this book, we wanted to make information readily available to anyone who wants to learn more about the basics of digital marketing. We hope that by reading this book, you have learned some foundational information about the basics — the fundamentals — of digital marketing.

The fundamentals of digital marketing that we presented in this book — a user-centered website, marketing fundamentals, market research, copywriting, pay per click advertising, tracking & analysis SEO, Social, UX Design, and Email Marketing — can work together to help you create a successful online presence. Each fundamental by itself can help you manage different aspects of your online presence, create relationships with existing customers, or gain new customers who are looking for what you have to offer.

When used together, however, these fundamentals can help your digital marketing succeed like a well-planned social event. No matter what industry your business is part of, these fundamentals can help create an interest in your brand, products and services that has not been there before.

See you at the top!